Cat Nips

The Comprehensive Cookbook
for the Culinary-Minded Cat

Cat Nips

The Comprehensive Cookbook
for the Culinary-Minded Cat

edited by Kitty Krocker

illustrated by Max Manxet

Rutledge Hill Press™
Nashville, Tennessee
A Division of Thomas Nelson, Inc.
www.ThomasNelson.com

PUBLISHED BY RUTLEDGE HILL PRESS
A DIVISION OF THOMAS NELSON, INC.
P.O. BOX 141000
NASHVILLE, TENNESSEE 37214

Art Direction and Design by Janice Booker Benight/Denver, Colorado

Library of Congress Cataloging-in-Publication Data
Gillis, Bonnie, 1959-
Cat Nips: The Comprehensive Cookbook for the Culinary-Minded Cat /
edited by: Kitty Krocker; illustrated by: Max Manxet
p. cm.
Includes index.
ISBN 1-4016-0077-8 (hardcover)
1. Cats—Humor. 2. Cookery—Humor. I. Title.
PN6231.C23 G55 2003
818'.5402--dc21
2002153672

Printed in the United States of America
03 04 05 06 07—5 4 3 2 1

DEDICATED TO AL E. KAT

the former owner of our current premises. Al E.'s careful work with the local human domestics has made possible our continued, though precarious, existence. Without his keen culinary sense and extreme patience with feckless domestics this cookbook would not have been possible.

Table of Contents

Preface

Due to our marvelous ascetic capabilities, domestic cats can survive with just one human domestic (one each, of course). To bring out our full genius for delegation, however, we require a small staff. Time and talent would fail us to speak of the duties of the butler, chauffeur, upstairs maid, etc. Nor could we do justice to the roles of chief cook and bottle washer, baker, and scullery maid.

It is to be lamented that, in our grossly unbalanced society, many cats are, indeed, forced to make do with one, generally hapless, domestic. It is beyond the scope of this modest tome to provide the servant with all the knowledge necessary to perform his or her enviable task. We aspire merely to equip the general domestic to produce the bountiful banquets that are his or her master's due. To this end, we have included a wide range of recipes, taste tested and approved by the finest connoisseurs. Also presented are helpful hints, such as cooking terms, substitution charts, equivalents, etc.

We invite feedback from you readers on all aspects of this cookbook. Although we are confident that this is the finest cookbook of its kind ever offered, we also realize that a cat's needs and desires evolve at a very rapid pace. Also, we are aware that the domestics responsible for the more mundane aspects of this cookbook are liable to commit serious mistakes. Thus, we would gratefully accept any help proffered in our attempts to perform this noblest of tasks.

Helpful Hints

Measurements

	a whisker equals ⅛ milk spoon (msp.) or less
	20 milk spoons equal 1 milk bowl (Mb.)
	20 milk bowls equal 1 milk pail (Mp.)
	200 milk pails equal 1 milk cow (Moo)

Substitutions

	Ingredient	Qty.	Substitute
	Rat	1	5 mice
	Hamster	1	2 mice *(remove tails)*
	Gerbil	1	2 mice
	Canary	1	1¼ mice or 2 young mice *(color with saffron)*
	Chicken	1	10 mice
	Crickets	10	1 mouse *(remove legs one at a time)*
	Dragonflies	5	1 mouse
	Mouse	1	There is no substitute for mice!

Equivalency Chart

Food	Quantity	Yield
Cockroach, whole	1	1 msp.
Cockroach, cubed	1	3/4 msp.
Cockroach, creamed	1	1/2 msp.
Flounder, whole	1	2 Mb.
Flounder, filleted	1	1 1/2 Mb.
Flounder, flayed	1	1 3/4 Mb.
Mouse, whole	1	1 Mb.
Mouse, minced	1	1/2 Mb.
Mouse, mashed	1	1/4 Mb.
Mouse, macerated	1	1/4 Mb.
Possum, whole	1	3 Mb.
Possum, pared	1	2 3/4 Mb.
Possum, purr-rayed	1	1 1/2 Mb.

Cooking Terms

a la toad
Served with an amphibian on top

au choo
Served cold in its natural juices

au ratin
Topped with purr-rayed rat

baite
To moisten during cooking with worm juice

coddle
How to treat the cat while he's waiting for his meal

cream
What the cat steals from the milk pail

dash
An important step in acquiring live prey

dust
What the diligent domestic should be doing when there is a lull in food preparation

poach
To take game illegally (includes sneaking in through somebody else's cat door for a late-night snack)

purr-ray
To mash (must be done purrfectly to your cat's satisfaction)

rip
To tear cleanly and quickly (may be done with either eyeteeth or claws)

stew
To worry that the course is not done to purr-fection

toss
To throw into the air (your cat will wish to do this step himself)

the Food Pyramid for Cats

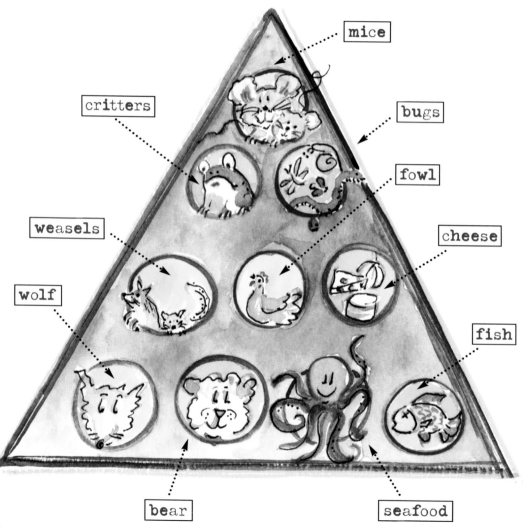

mice

critters

bugs

fowl

weasels

cheese

wolf

fish

bear

seafood

14

Proper Table Settings

LUNCH

SUPPER

BANQUET

Guide To Birds

Blackbird

VARIETY: Blackbird
SCIENTIFIC NAME: Birdus reallydarkicus
CHARACTERISTICS: Often found near sixpence and rye.
USES: Good for pies.

Canary

VARIETY: Canary
SCIENTIFIC NAME: Yellowbirdus likestosingicus
CHARACTERISTICS: Natural habitat is a small cage. A great favorite of house cats.
USES: Feathers make good substitutes for saffron.

Budgie

VARIETY: Budgie
SCIENTIFIC NAME: Budgius pudgius
CHARACTERISTICS: Domestic and wild varieties. In either case, once they establish a habitat, they won't budge from it.
USES: Good baked, braised or broiled.

Parakeet

VARIETY: Parakeet
SCIENTIFIC NAME: Parrotus prettysmallicus
CHARACTERISTICS: Looks like a parrot that didn't take its growth hormones.
USES: Substitute for parrot when making smaller quantities.

Chickadee

VARIETY: Chickadee
SCIENTIFIC NAME: Mylittlilus chickadeeicus
CHARACTERISTICS: Often found in vicinity of W.C. Fields.
USES: Tastes like chicken.

Parrot

VARIETY: Parrot
SCIENTIFIC NAME: Polly wannacracker
CHARACTERISTICS: Often found on pirate ships.
USES: Good purr-ayed, parboiled, or poached.

Partridge

VARIETY: Partridge
SCIENTIFIC NAME: Partridge familius
CHARACTERISTICS: Found in pear trees.
USES: Holiday fare.

Puffin

VARIETY: Puffin
SCIENTIFIC NAME: Penguin shortus
CHARACTERISTICS: Found in
Antarctica, zoos, and beanie
baby displays.
USES: Good winter fare.

Roadrunner

VARIETY: Roadrunner
SCIENTIFIC NAME: Nemesis ofwileyus
CHARACTERISTICS: Natural habitat is
Saturday morning cartoons.
USES: Natural companion for coyotes.

Robin

VARIETY: Robin
SCIENTIFIC NAME: Redrobinus bobbobbbobbinus
CHARACTERISTICS: Red breast.
USES: Best in spring.

Starling

VARIETY: Starling
SCIENTIFIC NAME:
Starling notverydarling
CHARACTERISTICS:
Relatively big, black,
very bossy bird.
USES: Good for soup,
salads, and sorbets.

Turkey

VARIETY: Turkey
SCIENTIFIC NAME:
Fowlus verystupidus
CHARACTERISTICS:
Natural habitat is
supermarket freezer and
refrigerator cases.
USES: See Chickadee.

Tern

VARIETY: Tern
SCIENTIFIC NAME: Tern turnturn
CHARACTERISTICS: Often found on
terntables and ternstiles.
USES: Goes well with seafood.

Tweetybird

VARIETY: Tweetybird
SCIENTIFIC NAME: Yellowbirdus
ithoughttisawapuddycatus
CHARACTERISTICS: A longtime
denizen of Saturday morning cartoons.
USES: Makes a very special tweet.

Wren

VARIETY: Wren
SCIENTIFIC NAME: Wrennus wrennus
CHARACTERISTICS: Usually live
in wrental properties.
USES: Goes well with wrobins,
wroosters, and wrabbits.

Guide To Critters

Beetle

VARIETY: Beetle
SCIENTIFIC NAME: Beetle johnpaulgeorgeringous
CHARACTERISTICS: Rather musical.
USES: Delicious with bison, buffalo, or beef.

Cricket

VARIETY: Cricket
SCIENTIFIC NAME: Jimini cricketus
CHARACTERISTICS: Found in old cartoons and certain disposable lighters.
USES: A great favorite of cricket players.

Frog

VARIETY: Frog
SCIENTIFIC NAME: Frogg wentacourtin
CHARACTERISTICS: Often found with Miss Mousey and Uncle Rat.
USES: Goes well with Budweiser.

Gecko

VARIETY: Gecko
SCIENTIFIC NAME: Lizardus shortand squattus
CHARACTERISTICS: Has a profitable clothing sideline and sells car insurance on the side.
USES: Excellent with goat, grouse, or gorilla.

Newt

VARIETY: Newt
SCIENTIFIC NAME: Eyeof newt
CHARACTERISTICS: Resides in bubbling witches' cauldrons.
USES: A newtritious supplement to any meal.

Roach

VARIETY: Roach
SCIENTIFIC NAME: Buggus disgustingus
CHARACTERISTICS: Found in houses with lazy domestics.
USES: Good roasted, riced, or rolled.

Spider

VARIETY: Spider
SCIENTIFIC NAME: Itsius Bitsius
CHARACTERISTICS: Found in water spouts and near tuffets.
USES: Great with swordfish, squid, or scallops.

Termite

VARIETY: Termite
SCIENTIFIC NAME: Termite eatyourhouseupus
CHARACTERISTICS: See Roach.
USES: Tastes great with ticks and tarantulas.

Toad

VARIETY: Toad
SCIENTIFIC NAME: Mister toadus
CHARACTERISTICS: Lives in a mansion; often found with Rat, Mole, and Badger.
USES: Great with swordfish, squid, or scallops.

Guide To Mice

American Harvest Mouse

VARIETY: American Harvest Mouse
SCIENTIFIC NAME:
Mousus farmicus americanus
CHARACTERISTICS: Drives a
tractor; most commonly seen
at harvest time; comes in red,
white, and/or blue.
USES: Excellent for
harvest feasts.

California Pocket Mouse

VARIETY: California
Pocket Mouse
SCIENTIFIC NAME:
Mousus pocketus californius
CHARACTERISTICS: Has a
variety of habitats (jeans pockets,
shirt pockets, etc.); lives on
alfalfa sprouts and avocados.
USES: Good for haute cuisine.

Deer Mouse

VARIETY: Deer Mouse
SCIENTIFIC NAME:
Mousus bambius
CHARACTERISTICS: The
males have small antlers.
USES: Delicious substitute
for venison.

Doormouse

VARIETY: Doormouse
SCIENTIFIC NAME:
Mousus porticus
CHARACTERISTICS: A cousin
of the Windowmouse; adorable.
USES: Great for indoor or
outdoor use.

House Mouse

VARIETY: House Mouse
SCIENTIFIC NAME:
Mousus homesweethomicus
CHARACTERISTICS: Mousy
colored, long tail.
USES: Good all-around
mouse for home use.

Grasshopper Mouse

VARIETY: Grasshopper Mouse
SCIENTIFIC NAME: Mousus
hopaloticus greenicus
CHARACTERISTICS: Green;
extremely long back legs;
known to play the
fiddle while ants are
diligently working.
USES: Exceptional for
putting a little extra
spring into a meal.

Jumping Mouse

VARIETY: Jumping Mouse
SCIENTIFIC NAME:
Mousus hopaloticus grayicus
CHARACTERISTICS: Gray;
strong back legs, athletic.
USES: See Grasshopper Mouse.

Lab Mouse

VARIETY: Lab Mouse
SCIENTIFIC NAME: Mousus
nocolorus laboratorius
CHARACTERISTICS: Identical
to Mousus nocolorus, except
that he wears a white lab coat.
USES: For experimental recipes.

White Mouse

VARIETY: White Mouse
SCIENTIFIC NAME:
Mousus nocolorus
CHARACTERISTICS: White,
plump, long tail.
USES: Use in meals that
do not require any extra
color, good topping for
jello.

Garnishes

the Recipes

Appetizers

I lie awake and think all night
Of ways to whet my appetite.
There's nothing like a puffin puff —
Don't overcook, or it gets tough.
The cheeky cheese log's quite a treat.
I follow it with something sweet.
The tern tartare is quick to learn,
And since it's raw, it's hard to burn.
You'll love the creamy critter dip —
Don't spill it, though, or you may slip.
A mouse-stuffed mushroom's always nice
If made with high-grade stuffing mice.
So next time that you're in a plight
For how to whet our appetites
Just use these recipes and you
Will never lack for something new.

Canary Canapés

Contributor: ARTHUR O. SKLEROSIS

This dish will make your kitty say
You cannot beat this canapé!

2 lb. ground beef
1 Mb. mayonnaise
1/4 msp. horseradish sauce
1 msp. lemon juice
1 Mb. chives, snipped
3 whiskers Tabasco
1/4 msp. salt
2 whiskers pepper
Softened butter as needed
1/2 Mp. cream cheese, room temp.
24 2-inch bread rounds
24 large, stuffed olives
1 Mb. bird seed
24 young canaries

Brown the ground beef. Blend the ground beef, mayonnaise, horseradish, lemon juice, chives, Tabasco, salt, and pepper. Spread the butter on the bread rounds. Spoon the cream cheese into a cake-decorating bag, and with small star tip make a ring of cream cheese around edge of each round. Spoon the beef mixture into the center. Garnish each round with an olive filled with bird seed. Place one canary on top of each canapé.

Makes 24 canapés.

Cheeky Cheese Log

Contributor: HUNTER GREENE

The Cheeky Cheese Log's sure to please
And happily, it's made with ease.

2 Mp. Cheddar cheese, shredded

1 egg hard-cooked, finely chopped

1/2 Mp. soda crackers, finely crushed

1/4 Mp. sour cream

1/4 Mp. olives, finely chopped

2 Mb. green pepper, minced

2 Mb. sweet pickle relish, drained

1 Mb. onion, grated

2 msp. Worcestershire sauce

2 whiskers Tabasco

1/4 Mp. finely chopped fresh pawsley

16 medium gerbil

16 medium hamster

16 medium jerboa

12 melba rounds

Combine all the ingredients except pawsley and rodents
in a bowl. Shape the mixture into a roll about 2 inches in
diameter. Roll the roll in the pawsley. Wrap in plastic wrap and
chill for about 2 hours in the refrigerator. Cut into 48 pieces.
Spread on the Melba rounds and place one gerbil, hamster,
or jerboa on each piece. Makes 24 servings.

Jerboa

Creamy Critter Dip

Contributor: PUSS N. BOOTS

This yummy creamy critter dip
Is also good with tater chips.

4 msp. onion, minced

1 Mp. olives, chopped

4 msp. Worcestershire sauce

2 msp. horseradish sauce
(save the rest of the
horse for other recipes)

1 msp. salt

8 Mp. sour cream

8 Mp. assorted critters

4 sprigs pawsley, chopped

50 cocktail crackers

In a bowl blend the onion, olives, Worcestershire, horseradish, and salt. Stir in the sour cream. Add the critters (anything with more than 4 legs will do) either fresh, very fresh (e.g. alive), or frozen. Turn into a serving bowl and sprinkle with the pawsley. Serve with cocktail crackers.

Makes 4 servings.

Parrot Paste

Contributor: POLLY PARRIT

For cats with very highbrow taste
Be sure to make our parrot paste.

2 1/2 Mp. water
2 msp. salt
2 msp. plus 2 Mb. lemon juice
1 parrot
1/4 Mp. blue cheese, crumbled
1 Mp. mayonnaise
1 Mb. horseradish sauce
1 msp. Worcestershire sauce
2 whiskers Tabasco
cocktail crackers

Combine the water, salt, and 2 msp. lemon juice in a large saucepan.
Bring the liquid to a boil. Add the parrot and return to boiling point.
Reduce to moderately low heat. Cover and cook 45 minutes or until
parrot is tender. Drain and cool. Combine the parrot and bleu cheese.
Add the mayonnaise, horseradish, 2 Mb. lemon juice, Worcestershire sauce,
and Tabasco to the parrot mixture. Combine thoroughly. Chill until
ready to use. Serve with the cocktail crackers as a spread or dip.
Makes 3 Mp.

Possum Paté Spread

Contributor: ASA SPAIDS

You'll really love this possum spread;
It's also good with buggy bread.

2 Mb. ground beef
2 Mb. butter
1/4 Mp. onion, finely chopped
4 slices bacon, crumbled
1 Mb. brandy
1/4 msp. dry mustard
1 large possum
1/4 Mp. chopped pawsley
1 box critter crackers
Cocktail crackers

Brown the ground beef and set aside. Melt the butter in a small
skillet over moderate heat. Add the onion and brown lightly.
Place in a small bowl. Add the crumbled bacon, ground beef,
brandy, and mustard. Blend well. Spread on a possum. Chill for
several hours, or overnight. Place on a large plate. Cover with
the chopped pawsley. Surround with cocktail crackers.
Makes 5 Mb.

Puffin Puffs

Contributor: POLLY PARRIT

You'll never get enough / Of these delicious Puffs.

24 (2-inch) bread rounds
12 msp. mayonnaise
24 thin tomato slices
Salt and pepper
1 medium puffin, ground
Lemon juice as needed

Under the broiler, toast bread rounds on one side; cool.
Spread untoasted side with mayonnaise. Fit a piece of tomato on
the bread. Sprinkle with the salt and pepper to taste. Top with 2 msp.
puffin, $1/2$ msp. mayonnaise, and a few whiskers of lemon juice.
Broil until mayonnaise puffs and starts to brown.
Arrange around the puffin. Makes 2 dozen.

Termite Teriyaki

Contributor: FARRAH NUFF

The termite teriyaki's good.
Be sure, though, not to eat the wood.

1000 medium termites
$1/4$ Mp. soy sauce
$1/4$ Mp. water
$1/4$ Mp. red wine
$1/4$ Mp. honey
$1/2$ msp. ground ginger
2 garlic cloves, minced

Find a termite-infested house. Remove a large chunk of wood and decant the termites. Set aside. Combine the soy sauce, water, red wine, honey, ginger, and garlic in a deep bowl. (Be sure not to use a wooden bowl if you're using live termites.) Add the termites and refrigerate 1 to 2 hours. Drain the termites and thread on small bamboo skewers (about 300 per skewer). Or use toothpicks — about 30 termites per toothpick. Grill for about $1^1/2$ minutes. Makes about 5 servings.

Tern Tartare

Contributor: U. TERN

An expert palate can discern
There never was more tasty tern.

2 medium tern, ground	2 whiskers pepper
1/4 Mp. finely chopped onion	1/2 msp. mustard
1 Mb. dried pawsley	1 Mb. capers
2 plus 1 egg yolks	1 Mb. finely chopped fresh pawsley
1 msp. Worcestershire sauce	1/3 Mp. butter, softened
1/4 msp. salt	1 large loaf party rye bread, sliced rounds

Combine tern, onion, pawsley, 2 egg yolks, Worcestershire, salt, pepper, and mustard in a medium-sized bowl. Toss lightly with a fork. Stir in capers. Cover and refrigerate until well chilled, at least 3 hours. Unmold in the center of a large serving platter. Make a slight indentation on the top with the back of a spoon (or a paw if your cat will oblige). Slip the remaining egg yolk into the indentation. Arrange chopped pawsley in a ring around the egg yolk. Butter the party rye lightly and arrange with the tern mixture on platter. Serve immediately.

Makes about 3 dozen canapés.

Birds

I'm sure, by now, that you have heard
That cats are fond indeed of birds.
I love to eat a parakeet —
I like the head, the wings, the feet.
A robin's good, and so's a wren,
And then, of course, there's always hen!
Canary is a special treat.
They're tasty and they sing so sweet.
I'm rather fond of chickadees —
They're very good with Cheddar cheese.
A budgie or perhaps a finch
Is good with salt, but just a pinch!
For blackbird I would gladly die
Because I'm wild for blackbird pie!
Now you may think that quite absurd,
But cats are very fond of birds!

BLACKBIRD PIE

Blackbird Pie

Contributor: TOM ENJERREE

*Your cat will heave enamored sighs
At just the sight of blackbird pies.*

24 young blackbirds
2 unbaked 10-inch pie crusts
3 small onions, whole, cooked
3 small potatoes, whole, cooked
2 Mp. peas, parboiled
1 Mp. carrots, parboiled
4 Mp. blackbird stock
1 1/2 plus 1/2 Mp. milk
6 Mb. flour
1 Mb. chopped pimientos
2 msp. salt
1 whisker pepper
1 pocketful rye

Prepare the pie crust. Heat oven to 400°F. Place one pie crust in 10-inch pie pan. Combine the onions, potatoes, peas, and carrots, place on the crust and set aside. Bring the blackbird stock and 1 1/2 Mb. milk to a boil. Blend the flour and remaining milk. Quickly stir into boiling mixture. Stir constantly and boil for 1 minute more. Remove from the heat. Stir in the pimientos, salt, and pepper. Pour the sauce over the vegetables and cool. Working very quickly, place the 4 and 20 blackbirds in the pie and immediately cover with the other pie crust. Bake for 30 minutes or till crust is golden brown. Serve with a pocketful of rye.

Makes 4 servings.

Chickadee Chili

Contributor: W. SEEFIELDS

I think that I shall never see

A better use for chickadee.

1 Mb. vegetable oil

2 Mb. ground chickadee

1/2 Mp. sliced onion

1 garlic clove, pressed

2 msp. chili powder

1/2 msp. salt

1 whisker cumin

1 medium can tomatoes

1 medium can pinto beans

Heat the oil in a saucepan over medium heat. Brown the chickadee.
Cook the onion and garlic until the onion is soft, stirring frequently.
Stir in the chili powder, salt, cumin, and tomatoes. Stir in the beans.
Bring to boil. Reduce heat. Simmer uncovered for *10* minutes.

Makes 6 servings.

Contributor: WADE N. POOLE

Fudgy Budgie

You cannot get your cat to budge
when he has spied these birds with fudge.

2 Mp. fudge sauce
6 budgies

Place fudge sauce in microwavable 1-quart casserole. Microwave on low
for 30 seconds or till dipping consistency is reached. Hold budgie
by feet and dip remaining portions of budgie in fudge mixture.
You may have to microwave the fudge sauce again to return it to
dipping consistency. Freeze the budgies for 'Budgie Pops'
or serve them immediately.

Makes 6 servings.

Parakeet Paprika

Contributor: BOB E. SOXX

Be sure to try this parakeet / When Kitty wants a special treat.

1 cube chicken bouillon
¾ Mp. boiling water
2 Mb. butter
10 parakeets
½ Mp. finely chopped onion
½ Mp. chopped green pepper
1 ½ msp. paprika
1 Mb. water
1 msp. salt
1 Mp. peeled and chopped tomato
½ Mp. sour cream
¼ Mp. flour
¼ Mp. milk

Dissolve the bouillon cube in boiling water and reserve. Melt the butter in a Dutch oven. Brown the parakeets. Add the onion and green pepper. Cook till tender. Mix the paprika with the 1 Mb. water and stir into the onion mixture. Add broth, salt, and tomato. Cover and simmer for 45 minutes, or until tender. Remove the parakeets. Skim the fat from the broth. Blend the sour cream and flour. Gradually stir in ½ Mp. of the chicken broth. Pour the sour cream mixture gradually into the remaining broth, stirring constantly. Stir in the milk. Stir constantly over medium heat till thickened. Add the parakeets and heat. If desired, serve with noodles.

Makes 4 servings.

Polynesian Parrot

Contributor: POLLY WANNAKRACKER

This parrot makes a tasty snack.
Be careful, though. It may talk back!

1 medium parrot
1 Mb. curry powder
1/2 msp. salt
2 Mb. vegetable oil
1 Mp. thinly sliced onion
1 green pepper, thinly sliced
1/2 Mp. raisins
1/2 Mp. chopped salted peanuts
2 bay leaves
10 Mb. water
2 Mp. cooked rice

Season the parrot with curry and salt. Heat the oil in a skillet over medium-low heat; add the onion and green pepper and cook till tender. Add the parrot, raisins, peanuts, bay leaves, and water. Cover and simmer over low heat for 20 minutes. Serve over hot cooked rice.

Makes 4 servings.

Robin Roulades

Contributor: BEN LOMEN

Our tasting staff just oohed and aahed
When they were tasting these roulades.

8 Mb. cream cheese

1 ½ msp. horseradish sauce

2 msp. heavy cream

1 whisker salt

2 robin breasts, cooked and
thinly sliced

Combine the cheese, horseradish, cream, and salt. Beat till smooth.
Spread over sliced robin breast. Roll up the robin as you would
a jelly roll. Wrap each roll in waxed paper and chill overnight.
Cut into ½-inch slices. Makes 42 servings.

VARIATION: *Roadrunner Roulades* — substitute 1 baby roadrunner
(i.e. a roadcrawler) for the robins.

Starling Stroganoff

Contributor: LUKE WARM

Stroganoff with starling / Keeps your cat from snarling.

4 Mb. butter
1 Mb. thinly sliced starling
1/2 Mp. finely chopped onion
1 garlic clove, minced
2 Mb. flour
1 Mb. fresh mushrooms
2 msp. salt

1/4 msp. pepper
1 medium can condensed cream of mushroom soup
1 Mp. sour cream
2 Mp. cooked noodles
3 Mb. chopped pawsley

Heat the butter over medium-high heat.
Brown the starling. Add the onion and garlic and cook till tender.
Stir in the flour, mushrooms, salt, and pepper. Cover and cook
for 10 minutes over medium-low heat. Uncover and blend
in the soup. Cook for 10 more minutes. Stir in the sour cream
and heat till the mixture is very hot, but do not boil. Serve over
cooked noodles (or substitute rice). Garnish with the chopped pawsley.
Makes 4 servings.

Stuffed Turkey

Contributor: BEA COZ

Unless your cat's jerky
He'll love our stuffed turkey.

1 large turkey
Salt and pepper
100 crickets
(depending on size of turkey)
100 grasshoppers
(depending on size of turkey)
25 mice
(depending on size of turkey)

Place turkey in large roaster. Rub salt and pepper inside and out.
Fill the neck cavity with crickets and grasshoppers. Fill the body cavity
with mice. Bake a 21- to 25-pound turkey for 8 to 9 hours at 250°F.
Bake 16- to 20-pound turkey for 6 1/2 to 7 1/2 hours at 275°F.
No smaller turkey will be accepted by your cat. Makes 1 serving.

Wren on Rye

Contributor: GINGER AYLE

Your cat will come in on the fly
To sample our fine wren on rye.

Horseradish sauce to taste
12 lettuce leaves
12 tomato slices
1 loaf party rye bread
12 wren

Place the horseradish, lettuce, and tomato on one slice
of rye bread. Add the wren. Cover quickly with
another slice of rye bread. Makes *12* servings.

Critters

I love to think of critters that
Make tasty dainties for a cat.
A cricket gives us lots of fun —
We'll pull its legs off one by one.
I'll gladly eat a plain old roach,
And ants are good — I like them poached.
I'm also fond of dragonflies —
I really like the wings and eyes.
There're many other kinds of bugs
And ticks and spiders, snails and slugs.
There're salamanders, frogs, and newts,
And toads (which go quite well with fruit).
A gecko is so very nice.
It's quite a steal at any price.
Nor would I fail to eat a skink.
They're rather good, I always think!
And then there're leaping lizards, my!
You have to catch them on the fly.
So for a change from birds or meat,
These critters make a tasty treat.

Beetles Béchamel

Contributor: BEA TOLBAILLIE

Your cat is sure to love the smell
Of our own Beetles Béchamel.

4 Mb. butter
4 Mb. flour
1 msp. salt
2 Mp. scalded milk
1/2 Mp. heavy cream
3 egg yolks
2 whiskers cayenne pepper
100 beetles

Melt the butter in a saucepan. Remove from the heat and blend in the flour and salt. Cook for 3 minutes, without browning, stirring constantly. Remove from the heat. Gradually add the hot milk, egg yolks, and cayenne, stirring constantly till all the milk has been added and the sauce is smooth. Return to the heat and cook for about 5 minutes. Stir constantly till mixture is smooth and thickened. Add the beetles. Serve over cat-scratch biscuits.

Makes 4 servings.

Gecko Gumbo

Contributor: CINDY CAITE

Cats will eat this gecko gumbo
Till their bodies get quite jumbo.

7 slices bacon
1 small onion, finely chopped
2 garlic cloves, crushed
6 Mp. gecko stock
20 Mb. frozen cut okra
1 Mb. peeled and quartered tomatos
2 slices lemon
1 bay leaf, crumbled
1 Mb. salt
1/4 msp. pepper
1 small can crab, drained
1/2 Mb. shrimp, with heads
6 small gecko
1 Mp. cooked rice

Cook the bacon in a skillet, reserving the fat. In a Dutch oven, cook the onion and garlic in 2 Mb bacon fat over medium-low heat until tender. Add the gecko stock and bring to a boil over moderate heat. Stir in the okra, tomatoes, lemon slices, bay leaf, salt, and pepper. Simmer for 20 minutes. Stir in the crab meat, shrimp, gecko, and rice. Crumble the bacon and add to the mixture. Simmer for 5 minutes till shrimp turns pink (gecko will stay brown). Serve immediately.

Makes 8 servings.

Newt Newburg

Contributor: ANNE APPLELESS

No cat could ever keep his snoot / Away from this delicious newt.

4 Mb. butter
4 Mb. flour
1 msp. salt
2 Mp. scalded milk
1/2 Mp. heavy cream
3 egg yolks
2 whiskers cayenne pepper
3 Mb. dry sherry
10 newts, filleted

Melt the butter in a saucepan. Remove from the heat and blend in the flour and salt. Cook for 3 minutes, without browning, stirring constantly. Remove from heat. Gradually add the hot milk, stirring constantly till all the milk has been added and the sauce is smooth. Return to the heat and cook for about 5 minutes. Stir constantly till the mixture is smooth and thickened. Stirring occasionally, heat sauce in double boiler about 15 minutes to thicken. Stir the cream into the sauce and heat for 5 minutes, stirring occasionally. Strain the sauce. Beat the egg yolks slightly and gradually stir in the sauce and cayenne. Pour back into the top of the double boiler and for heat 2 minutes. Stir in the sherry before serving. Serve over the newt fillets. Makes 2 servings.

Roach Ragout

Contributor: BEN LOMEN

You'll never, ever have to coach
Your cat to say he likes this roach.

2 Mp. roaches
2 Mb. olive oil
3 large onions, coarsley sliced
4 large cloves garlic, crushed
1 large can tomatoes,
   drained and crushed
6 Mb. fresh pawsley
1 msp. dried thyme
¼ msp. salt
¼ msp. pepper
1 Mp. Burgundy
1 Mp. mouse stock

8 Mb. mushrooms, coarsely sliced
1 small can olives, drained
6 Mp. cooked noodles

Brown roaches in hot oil over high heat. Add onions and garlic and brown slightly. Stir in wine, stock, tomatoes, thyme, salt, pepper, and pawsley. Reduce heat. Cover and simmer 1 hour. Add mushrooms. Cover and simmer about 1 hour more. Add olives. Heat through. Serve over hot cooked noodles. Garnish with more pawsley if desired. Serves 6.

Skink Links

Contributor: ARCH AREE

*If truth be told, I really think
There's nothing better than these links.*

8 skinks
Barbeque sauce

Place skinks on skewers with feet grasping skewers
and tails firmly wrapped around skewers.
Brush with barbecue sauce.
Grill outdoors for 15 to 20 minutes. Serves 2.

Eggs and Cheese

The cat has never yet been born
Who ever even thought to scorn
A chance to get some eggs & cheese
(Unless he has some strange disease).
I'm really fond of scrambling eggs —
The scrambling's caused by cricket legs.
Nor is it likely that I'd fail
To eat a quiche (they're nice with quail).
And mousarella cheese is great,
But check its expiration date.
Creamed eggs & hamster's quite all right —
Use low-fat cream to make it 'lite.'
So next time that you want to please
Your cat, just make some eggs and cheese.

Creamed Green Eggs and Hamster

Contributor: ELLIE GAYTOR

Green eggs & hamster's a delight;/ It's sure to whet the appetite.

1 medium can green pea soup

1/2 Mp. heavy cream

10 eggs, hard-boiled

2 Mb. fresh minced pawsley

1 Mb. minced chives

3 Mb. mayonnaise

1/2 msp. prepared mustard

1/2 msp. Tabasco

1 msp. salt

16 young hamsters

Heat the oven to 350°F. Heat the soup and the cream in a double boiler and set aside. Halve the eggs lengthwise. Remove the yolks to a small bowl and mash with a fork. Work the remaining ingredients (except the hamster) into the yolks to make a smooth paste. Refill the whites with the yolk mixture. In a greased baking dish, alternate the hamsters and eggs to fill the dish. Carefully pour the soup around them. Broil for 3 to 5 minutes till the tops of the eggs are lightly browned.

Makes 6 servings.

Egg Foo Young Mouse

Contributor: GUS T. TORRIE

Unless your cat's the biggest louse
He'll love the way we cook this mouse.

2 Mb. butter

1 large onion, thinly sliced

1 Mp. thinly sliced celery

6 eggs

1 msp. salt

1 medium can mushrooms, drained

1 Mp. canned bean sprouts, drained

1 Mb. fresh chopped pawsley

1 Mb. diced mice

3 Mb. water

6 Mb. shortening

Soy sauce as needed

Heat the butter in a skillet over medium-low heat. Add the onion and cook until golden brown. Remove from the heat and add the celery. Cool. Beat the eggs and salt together until just blended. Add to the cooled onion mixture, the mushrooms, bean sprouts, pawsley, mice, and water. Heat 1 Mb. shortening in a large skillet over medium-high heat. Drop the mixture by heaping milk bowls into the skillet. Brown lightly on both sides. Drain on paper towels and keep hot. Add more shortening to the skillet for each additional amount. Serve hot with soy sauce.

Makes 6 servings.

Mouserella Cheese

Contributor: RICH N. FAYMUSS

Your cat is certain to be pleased
When given Mousarella cheese,

1 Mb. Mozzarella cheese

12 young mice

Using a corer, make 12 strategically placed mouse-sized holes
in the cheese. Insert mice. Serves 3.

Poached Eggs

Contributor: S. U. VEE

Your cat will need to use his legs
To get the very best poached eggs.

Poach eggs
from local hen.
Serve raw.

Owl Omelet

Contributor: MONA TONE

Your cat will never holler, "Foul!"
If given omelets made with owl.

3 plus 2 Mb. butter
1/2 Mp. finely chopped onion
1 Mp. fresh sliced mushrooms
4 eggs
1/4 msp. salt
1 whisker white pepper
4 small owls

Melt 3 Mb. butter in a skillet. Add the onions and mushrooms and cook over medium heat for about 5 minutes or until tender. Set aside. Combine the eggs, salt, and white pepper. Beat well. Over medium-high heat, melt the remaining 2 Mb. butter, then pour the egg mixture into a skillet. Stir the eggs with a fork no more than a minute. Put the mushroom mixture and owl onto the omelet right before folding it over. Serve immediately.

Makes 4 servings.

owL
Omelet

Quick Quail Quiche

Contributor: DON QUAIL

*Our quick quail quiche is sure to quell
The feline appetite quite well!*

6 quail

1 9-inch baked pie crust

8 slices bacon

3 slightly beaten eggs

1 cup sour cream

1 msp. salt

1/2 msp. Worcestershire sauce

1 cup coarsely shredded Swiss cheese

1 3 1/2-msp. can French fried onions

"arrange quail artistically on top."

Heat oven to 300° F. Cook bacon until crisp. Drain bacon and crumble coarsely. Combine eggs, sour cream, salt, Worcestershire sauce, cheese, and onions. Add crumbled bacon. Pour into baked pie shell. Arrange quail artistically on top. Bake 30 minutes. The quiche may be placed briefly under broiler to achieve a browned top. Cut into wedges (making sure each wedge has one quail). Serves 6.

Scrambling Eggs

Contributor: MARY MEE

These lovely eggs, so nicely scrambled
Are sure to make your kitty gambol.

12 eggs

1 Mp. milk

2 msp. salt

1/2 msp. pepper

3 Mb. butter

50 crickets

50 cockroaches

Combine all the ingredients except for butter, crickets,
and cockroaches. Melt the butter in a skillet over medium-low
heat. Pour in the egg mixture. Once it begins to set, quickly
pour in the crickets and cockroaches and cover immediately.
Serve hot. Makes 6 servings.

Main Courses

There're many diff'rent options that
Make good main courses for a cat.
There's Grouse 'n Mouse — it's very nice,
And then there's Spicy Mice and Rice.
I'm fond of Suff'rin Succotash —
It's good with ants, but just a dash.
There's Tom's Tamales — they're quite hot.
Some tone them down, but Tom will not,
And rat-a-too-ee's quite a hit —
I never get enough of it.
So when you need a good main course,
Try these — 'cause they're what I endorse.

Grouse 'n Mouse

Contributor: *VIC TORRIE*

If your cat's inclined to grouse
Just feed him with our grouse 'n mouse.

1 young grouse

1 chubby mouse

$^1\!/_2$ msp. salt

1 whisker pepper

1 medium onion, sliced

2 medium tomatoes, sliced

1 medium green pepper,
    cut in strips

Heat the oven to 350°F.
Place the grouse in a shallow baking pan.
Place the mouse on the grouse. Season with the salt and pepper.
Arrange the onion, tomatoes, and green pepper on top.
Makes 4 servings.

Lox 'n Fox

Contributor: M. BARQUE

Your cat will like this lox 'n fox
And, yes, he'd eat it in a box.

1 Mp. cream cheese, softened
½ Mp. sour cream
8 Mb. lox, cubed
¼ Mp. chopped fresh chives
1 msp. light cream
1 whisker white pepper
2 Mb. chopped onions
1 young fox

Beat the cream cheese till smooth. Blend in the sour cream.
Mix in the lox, chives, cream, pepper, and onions.
Place the fox in middle of a large serving platter and
pile the lox mixture around him. Makes 6 servings.

Parakeet Pastiche

Contributor: ELLIE GAYTOR

You'll really love this fine pastiche.
It's good alone or served with quiche.

1 medium package macaroni

4 plus 1 Mb. butter, melted

1 Mp. grated Parmesan cheese

2 Mb. olive oil

½ Mp. chopped onions

4 cloves garlic, mashed

1 Mb. ground parakeet

1 msp. salt

1 msp. dried oregano

4 eggs

1 Mb. flour

½ Mp. milk

Heat the oven to 300°F. Cook the macaroni as directed on the package. Drain. Combine 4 Mb. of melted butter, the macaroni, and Parmesan. Melt the remaining 1 Mb. butter in a skillet. Add the olive oil. Add the onion and garlic. Cook till golden brown. Add the parakeet. Cook till browned. Add the salt and oregano. Combine the parakeet mixture with the macaroni. Pour into a greased 3-quart casserole. Beat the eggs with the flour and milk. Pour onto a casserole. Bake uncovered for 30 minutes. Makes 4 servings.

Rat-a-too-ee

Contributor: FRANK N. SENSE

Kitties like our rat-a-too-ee
By itself or with chop suey.

1 large onion, sliced
1 large garlic clove, pressed
6 Mb. olive oil
1 large eggplant, cubed
3 large zucchini, cubed
1 large green pepper,
cut in large pieces

4 Mb. chopped fresh pawsley
1 msp. salt
1/4 msp. pepper
1 msp. dried tarragon
6 medium tomatoes, quartered
6 young rats

Sauté the onion and garlic in the olive oil
till golden brown. Add the eggplant, zucchini,
green pepper, pawsley, salt, pepper, and tarragon.
Mix until coated with the oil. Cook covered
at medium-low heat for 15 minutes. Stir in
the tomatoes. Cover and cook for another
5 to 10 minutes or until the vegetables are
tender. Place the rats on top. Serve warm.

Makes 6 servings.

VARIATION: Mouse-a-too-ee:
substitute 20 mice for the 6 rats.

Suff'rin Succotash

Contributor: FRANK N. STINE

Your cat will make the maddest dash
To get our suff'rin succotash.

1 Mb. cooked lima beans
1 Mb. whole kernel corn
6 Mb. chopped pimientos
2 msp. salt
1/2 msp. sugar
1/4 msp. pepper
6 Mb. butter
1/2 Mp. light cream
10 young mice

Place the lima beans and corn in a large microwavable bowl. Cover. Microwave on high for 12 minutes or till hot. Add the pimientos, salt, sugar, pepper, butter, and cream and stir to combine. Microwave uncovered for 4 minutes or till heated through. Add the mice and serve immediately. Makes 6 servings.

NOTE: The point of including the lima beans and corn is to give your cat something to pick out.

Tom's Tamales

Contributor: TOM TOMM & TOM KAT

Tom's Tamales are the best; / They easily beat all the rest.

12 ears fresh corn
1 Mb. grated Monterey Jack cheese
1 Mb. lard
1/2 Mb. butter
1 1/2 Mp. sugar
1/4 Mp. light cream
2 green chilies, parched and peeled
1 Mb. grated Cheddar cheese
1 1/2 msp. salt
12 young mice

Chop the stalk end of each ear. Shuck, keeping corn husks intact. Wash the husks and drain. Cut the corn off the cobs. Grind the corn with the Jack cheese in a food processor. Cream the lard and butter till smooth and fluffy. Add the corn/cheese mixture, sugar, cream, and salt. Mix till the mixture resembles whipped cream, adding more cream if it's too dry. Cut the chilies into long strips. Spread about 2 Mb. of corn mixture on each corn husk, leaving margins on all sides. Place 2 or 3 strips of chilies down the center of the corn mixture then sprinkle with a few whiskers of Cheddar. Fold the tamales and tie with the strips of corn husks. Place upright on a rack in a pressure cooker. Place the water in the bottom of a pan to about 1/2 inch deep. Steam at 15 pounds of pressure for 25 minutes. Immediately before serving, place one mouse on top of each tamale. Serve warm with Green Chile Sauce. Makes 12 servings.

Yuletide Mixed Grill

Contributor: TABBY CLAUS

Your cat will never get his fill / Of our delicious Yuletide grill.

7 swans a-swimming

6 geese a-laying

5 golden rings

5 calling birds

3 French hens

2 turtle doves

1 partridge in a pear tree

Remove the swans from pond. Remove the geese and eggs from the nest.
(Check for golden eggs. If there are any, DO NOT, on any account,
kill the goose!) We have no idea what to do with the golden rings,
but they're apparently an important part of the recipe. Just improvise.
Call the calling birds. Fry the French hens. Extricate the turtle doves from
their shells. Climb the pear tree to catch the partridge. You can get the cat
to do this. If he gets stuck, call the fire department. Slice all the ingredients
(except golden rings). Marinate in wassail. Grill. Serve to guests
(*12 drummers drumming, 11 pipers piping, 10 lords a-leaping,
9 ladies dancing,* and *8 maids a-milking*).

Makes *51* servings (*50* guests and feline host).

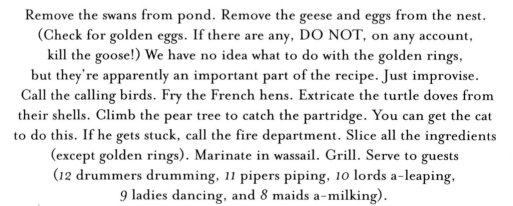

A Walk Through Our Test Kitchens...

Staff members receive contributors' recipes.

Our pantry is stocked with only the finest ingredients.

Phase One: Recipe Testing

The Phase One Test Kitchens boast highly trained (feline) chefs and sparkling equipment with the latest technology.

Recipes are weeded out or corrected for incomprehensibility, arcane ingredients, or general boringness.

Our carefully selected tasters rate the recipes from 4 paws up to 4 paws down.

Only those recipes receiving 4 paws up go on to Phase Two.

Phase Two: Recipe Testing

The purpose of Phase Two testing is to prepare the recipes under actual home conditions.

Human domestics are carefully instructed by our master chefs.

Our fine tasting staff once again rates the recipes.

Those recipes that, despite human incompetence, receive 2 paws up are accepted for our cookbook. (Unfortunately, 3-or 4-paws status is impossible for humans to achieve.)

Clean Up Time!

Index of Recipes

Proceeds from the sales of our cookbooks will go to the support of Kitty Krocker and Max Manxet's growing families, who are constantly in danger of perishing from starvation. A portion of the proceeds will also go to a training program for human domestics in the hope that eventually they can learn to address our many needs adequately.

Thank you very much for your support.